FOLLOWING JESUS TODAY

stories and reflections

Edited by Rob Fennell

FOLLOWING JESUS TODAY: Stories and Reflections

Edited by Rob Fennell
Published by Robert C. Fennell
November 2023
Halifax, Nova Scotia

ISBN: 978-1-7772394-4-2 (paperback)
       978-1-7772394-3-5 (e-book)

Cover image (photo of cross) by Vaishakh Pillai, India (Unsplash). Used, with thanks, by permission of the artist. Cover design by Rob Fennell.

Frontispiece (Matthew 23:11) by Helen Siegl. Used, with thanks, by permission of the Helen Siege Estate and the Siegl Family.

Quotations from the Bible are taken from the New Revised Standard Version
© 1989 Thomas Nelson.

All rights reserved. This book or parts thereof may not be reproduced in any form, stored in any retrieval system, or transmitted in any form by any means—electronic, mechanical, photocopy, recording, or otherwise—without prior written permission of the Author(s), with the exception of short passages cited in criticism or review.

The moral rights of the Authors and the Editor have been asserted.
Send notice of errata to the Editor.

Each entry in this volume is © 2023 The Authors. Please respect the Authors' copyright. Contact individual authors for permission to reprint. Authors have the right to reproduce, share, or sell copies of this work at their discretion.

TABLE OF CONTENTS

Foreword 6

1 The World Needs More Jesus
Sara Jewell 12

2 On Being a Loving Presence
Hugh Farquhar 20

3 Adulting 2.0
Michelle Robichaud 25

4 A Small Season
Heather Ferrier 29

5 Following Jesus to the Lowest Places
Frank Emanuel 33

6 Sink or Sail
Kimberly Heath 42

7 What It Means For Me To Follow Jesus
Joe Sharpe 47

8 The Rock
Penny MacDonald 49

9 In this world together
Kim McKellar 53

10 Following Jesus Together
   Heather Carlson 55

11 Jesus: Baggage, Blame, and Bathwater
   Jennifer Swanson 61

12 Down in the Valley with Jesus
   Susan Girard 67

13 Lead. Follow. Leave.
   Deborah Ambridge Fisher 75

14 Pews for Sale
   Heather Fletcher 81

15 Why I Follow Jesus Today
   William N. Drysdale 92

16 Walking with the Followers of Jesus, 1968-1990
   Tadashi (Tad) Mitsui 100

17 Al's having a baby!
   Allan David Smith-Reeve 110

An Invitation 120

Foreword

Somewhere in my travels in the cyberland of social media, I overheard (or "overread"?) a conversation about how mainline Christians can be quite shy about sharing their faith. They are not always forthcoming about expressing their spirituality with words, either aloud or in writing. Perhaps this is true for you, too.

Yet hearing one another's voices is an important way to understand how faith is lived in every generation.

With that idea in the back pocket of my mind, I started asking around to see if anyone might be interested in sharing a few words about their faith. It turns out that quite a few people were ready for this challenge. I suggested to these authors that they didn't need to comment on who Jesus was, or to get tangled up in theological quandaries. Mostly I was curious about what it looked like, in our generation, in this moment in history, to follow

Jesus. The theme of "following Jesus" seemed especially relevant. Focusing on "today" helps us see the faith of yesteryear visibly at work in the deep and personal realities of our own time, rather than falsely imagining that Christianity is an old, dead religion.

Speaking and writing about Jesus, and how we follow him, gives real substance to Christian faith. Christianity can't be reduced to a constellation of doctrines, a series of actions, or a cluster of inward attitudes and convictions. Actually following Jesus in everyday life, real life, a life like yours or mine, is the test of whether Christianity is truly the Way we have chosen.

In the Bible, we find Jesus healing, teaching, eating, drinking, walking, and challenging religious norms. Some perceive him to be a great leader, and others see him as a serious threat. When Jesus meets certain people, he tells them, "Follow me." He is building up a movement, perhaps.

It's a short, simply phrase: "Follow me." It's deceptively simple. For those of us who choose to follow him today, it's not simple at all. Many things and people and forces want our attention and our loyalty. The call to be "followers" of celebrities on social media, or advocates for certain brands of products, or to be part of political and social movements presses in on us every day. And without even noticing it, we are often deeply focused on our own priorities, agendas, and wishes. It's more straightforward to follow ourselves that to follow Jesus.

In the midst of all that, Jesus still says, "Follow me."

To my great delight, the authors whose work appears in this little book offer us vulnerable, joyful, moving, and personal expressions of following Jesus today. My deep thanks goes out to them, not only for contributing to the book, but also for their longsuffering patience as I was the cause of delaying this publication more than once.

In this book, you'll find stories, anecdotes, reflections, original artwork, and poetry. You'll find everyday experiences and extraordinary moments here. I hope you enjoy it. I hope it will be an inspiration to you as you reflect on following Jesus yourself, and what that means to you. And I hope that it blesses your own discoveries and delight along the Way of Jesus.

Rob Fennell

1

The World Needs More Jesus

Sara Jewell

In my work as a lay worship leader, I first used the expression, "The world needs more Jesus," in a church message in October 2016. The day's scripture reading was the story of Jesus healing a man possessed by demons, and this is what Jesus said to the man after he healed him: *"Return to your home, and declare how much God has done for you."*

Go and tell your story.

My message for that Sunday was about storytelling, and how storytelling is a basic human instinct. (I also work as a substitute teacher. A classroom full of chatty seven-year-olds is undeniable proof that telling stories is our irrepressible way of finding a path through the world.) We need to tell our own story and we need to listen to other stories because it's how we come to understand ourselves and each other.

Storytelling creates unity and empathy; it creates understanding and acceptance. Storytelling is the way Jesus created disciples, and it's the way we become his followers. In that 2016 message, I wrote, "Jesus was a revolutionary, and if we follow him, we need to follow his way: to be radical and obvious and outspoken in order to remind the world, and the church, why we follow Jesus, and why the world needs more Jesus."

That line—the world needs more Jesus—hit the tuning fork in my heart and it hasn't stopped vibrating since. It's why I want more stories about Jesus, why I want more of his stories.

It's how I became a follower of Jesus.

Eventually.

The path I walked is a long and winding one, littered with stories that didn't make sense, stories I didn't understand, stories I didn't know how to tell—until I tripped over a rock in my path and tumbled into lay worship leadership.

I was born and raised in The United Church of Canada. The congregation of my childhood in the 1970s was vibrant and active, full of children and young people. My memories aren't of Sunday school, but of the weekend retreats at our local church camp, the Christmas Eve pageants, and the youth group's production of Marlo Thomas' Free To Be You and Me.

Perhaps more revealing, however, is that I often called the minister, "Jesus."

Garth couldn't have looked less like the long-haired, white-skinned Jesus with the patrician nose pictured in our books and hanging on our church walls. Garth had short, curly brown hair and he wore glasses.

Here's what else this five-year-old saw: Garth wore a long white gown and waved his arms around when he spoke. He was a dynamic speaker, passionate and animated. He also was a close family friend, and flooded our quiet lives with his energy and intelligence. He was particularly fond of our "Little Red Renault," the very cheap, very basic compact car my father bought my mother in 1972. It had a stick shift and Garth loved to drive it, borrowing it whenever his wife had their station wagon.

Some of this comes to me as a story. I don't actually remember these young years as clearly as I wish I did. But as a writer, I understand how deeply our memories reside, even if our conscious mind can't access them. I do believe that when I'm dying and my brain conjures up Jesus coming for me, it will be Garth in his white gown pulling up beside my bed in the Little Red Renault.

Despite these vibrant and compelling early influences, by the time I reached my teens, we lived in a different town and attended a completely different church. The ministers were dull, unrelatable, and uninspiring, easy to tune out. That's when I lost Jesus and his passion and energy for his message and mission. He was no longer at church. He was no longer in my life. It would be thirty years before I found him again.

My path to lay worship leadership is the

result of a detour set up by one of the rural United Churches listed in the "Church Notices" of the community newspaper for which I worked. It was my job to update the services and I noticed one church had a different minister listed every week. So I emailed my contact and told her I could provide a worship service or two whenever they needed someone. In rural Nova Scotia, however, ministers are scarce. My one or two services turned into a steady gig now in its ninth year.

To lay worship leadership I brought my skills as a journalist (researching and writing) and the mind of a faith seeker (doubting and questioning) who, like any good journalist, asked *Why?*

A lot.

Over time, one big question kept nagging at me: *Why are we still reading the Old Testament?* In my new journey creating worship services, it frustrated me that we have Jesus' new way and new truth, yet the stories in the Hebrew scriptures seemed to be given as much weight, if not more, than Jesus' stories and his one commandment. *Why?*

I wasn't raised in a Bible-thumping, Bible-reading, Bible-quoting family (unless you count my mother saying, "Get thee behind me, Satan," every time she held out her glass when offered more wine). Perhaps if I knew all those ancient stories about the people of Israel, if I'd been told they were important and essential, or better, poetic and metaphorical, universal and ageless, I might feel some attachment to them, some loyalty and devotion, a connection. But I wasn't.

This is part of the reason I couldn't finish an introductory course called Christian Theology. I became so annoyed at how the early church was constructed and the collection of scriptures manipulated that I knew there was no way I could do a traditional kind of theological degree. I wanted more Jesus, not less.

A few years later, I discovered that what is written about Jesus is a testament, but his message and mission were a *covenant*—a new agreement between God and humanity. Jesus is the new way of interacting with God, and with each other. *Love one another the way I have loved you*, Jesus said. *Be unified by this love.*

With that discovery, my rock-strewn, tangled path suddenly opened up to a bright, sunlit field. That's why I struggled to relate to the ancient stories. That's why I didn't know how to tell my own faith story. As soon as I started to think about Jesus as the new covenant, offering a new law based his commandments about love, it all made sense. I understood I wasn't the one who had lost the plot of the Jesus story; it was those who created the church who had misled us from the beginning. I grew up seeing Jesus alive and well, waving his arms in the sanctuary and driving my mother's car and picnicking in the park by the lake. I was raised with the idea of Jesus, the man, the minister, the teacher, the preacher. The guy who died every Easter but kept coming back, kept doing Jesus-y things, saying Jesus-y things—at church, yes, but also at the church camp and with the Christmas pageant and when my mother and Garth did their show on the local radio station. Jesus was all around, and he was busy. Christ is alive! Hallelujah!

That was enough for me. It still is.

The path opened up and I found Jesus again—in myself, rather than in someone else. Now I understand the stories. Now I can relate to the stories. I see the stories all around me, and see Jesus at work through others (and sometimes me), and know why I believe the world needs more Jesus.

Now I can go and tell my story with passion and energy.

Sara Jewell is the author of Alphabet of Faith (2021) and Field Notes: A City Girl's Search for Heart and Home in Rural Nova Scotia (2016). She works as a substitute teacher, and a licensed lay worship leader in The United Church of Canada. Born and raised in Ontario, Sara lives in rural Nova Scotia.

2

On Being a Loving Presence

Hugh Farquhar

I cite three occasions when the inclination to follow Jesus took hold of my consciousness.

The first happened when I was about fourteen, at Pinehurst summer church camp in Nova Scotia. Every evening, we gathered in the beautiful outdoor chapel by the river. Two of the leaders influenced me greatly, Rev. Whitney Dalrymple and Rev. Mac Harlow. Their commitment to Jesus was visible, as was their care for us boys. I remember thinking that if following Jesus means being like them, I want to follow. One evening at chapel I sang a solo. "Fairest Lord Jesus, thee will I cherish, thee will I honour . . ." I meant it.

The second happened as the result of a summer job while attending university. I was working as a counsellor at a residential school for mentally challenged children, then called the Nova Scotia Youth Training Centre. My job was to take care of the boys in the residence, supervising mealtimes, planning after- school activities, and generally being responsible for their safety and welfare. During that summer, I experienced a deep affection beamed at me by the children, which I reciprocated. I saw how some of them displayed an uncomplicated faith in Jesus.

Then I began to read the Gospels in earnest and to get in touch with Jesus in a more profound way. I could see that the love I had come to embrace was the love that Jesus had brought to the world, especially for those who lived outside humanly created boundaries. I concluded that love was indeed the key to life's mystery and meaning, and that the source of it could not be something on the periphery of my life.

The third transformative occasion happened several years later at a Holy Week worship service in J. Wesley Smith Memorial United

Church in Halifax, as we sang the hymn, *When I Survey the Wondrous Cross*. The words that captured my attention were, "Love so amazing, so divine, demands my soul, my life, my all." This marked the climax of an internal struggle with being first nudged periodically, and then frequently, toward something I had a strong urge to resist: the ministry of the Church. I did not know if I had gifts for it. Besides, at that time, I had other plans for my life.

So here I am, all these years later, looking back on those experiences (and others) with gratitude, because following Jesus has been and continues to be the joy of my life. I see a progression in the three experiences from allegiance, to love, to service. All three speak to me of what it means to follow Jesus.

It means looking to Jesus as the focal point in my life. The writer of Hebrews advises, to "keep our eyes fixed on Jesus." He uses a particular Greek word that means "to focus on without being distracted." One of my favourite contemporary hymns is *Three Things I Promise*.

It speaks to me of my ongoing allegiance when I sing my promise "to cling to Christ" day by day.

When I was in seminary, an evangelical preacher put a one-line message on his telephone and invited people to call in. He called it, "dial-a-prayer." For a joke, we used to give first-year students the number and say that a person had called and wanted them to call them back. I'm not proud of that now. But you know what? I remember one of those messages all these years later. That preacher we made fun of said this: "Christianity is of the heart. It is not of the mind." Does that mean you park your intellect at the door when you follow Jesus? Of course not. But he was right in saying that the fundamental thing is opening my heart to a person who showed me the meaning of love in action.

To me, following Jesus means being a loving presence in this world, especially for those who, like my charges at the Youth Training Centre, are often starving for affirmation. It means offering compassion and respect, being an ardent listener, and understanding without judging. It means to be in my time as Jesus was in his: a loving presence.

And to follow Jesus means to serve. In the Sermon on the Mount, Jesus said to his disciples, and now says to me, "You are salt; you are light." Salt does things! It halts corruption. It helps with healing. It adds flavour. Light does things. It dispels darkness. It uncovers lost things. It gives direction.

These images remind me that as a follower of Jesus. I am meant to be a doer of the Word. This was his way of teaching that faith is a verb, and that love issues forth in actions promoting peace with justice.

> *Hugh Farquhar identifies himself primarily as spouse to Claudette, father to four, grandfather to five, and great grandfather to four. He is Minister Emeritus at St. Paul's United Church, Riverview, New Brunswick. For the last thirty years, he has been a sessional instructor in Biblical Studies at Atlantic School of Theology.*

3

Adulting 2.0

Michelle Robichaud

When I was little, I loved following Jesus. I would attend church with a glad heart, wanting to know more about him. I would pray every day, having intimate conversations with him, telling him about my day, how I was feeling, and what I wanted.

I don't know what happened to change all that. Abruptly, in my teens, I stopped going to church and ceased having conversations with Jesus. It was not that I stopped believing in God. Rather, I felt the need to strike out on my own. What started out as a journey of self-discovery ended in a circling back to Jesus—and a greater understanding of myself and what God's purposes are for me than I ever could have imagined.

During my 20s and 30s, I resisted Jesus,

despite the constant invitation he issued to come back to him. In fact, I didn't recognize this invitation at first. It manifested itself as a vague ennui in the beginning. As the years went on, however, it became more insistent—it turned into an unsettling restlessness, and then a deep depression. When I finally recognized it for what it was and answered the call, the depression lifted, the restlessness disappeared, and the path became clear. That path has led to me back to the fold. And it has led me to ministry.

Following Jesus is life changing. I moved from my home in Ottawa to a small village in the Ottawa Valley to serve a congregation as their student minister. My life has been turned upside down—I changed from a career to a vocation, I left my friends for a place where I knew no one, and I jumped into a challenging education, decades after completing university. What's more, I've never looked back. Jesus has taken care of me the entire way. I love living here, I love ministry, and I love school. I no longer feel trapped or restless or disconnected. I feel, for the first time since I was a child, *safe*.

Following Jesus is not easy. It takes a great relationship with him. It takes trust. And it takes humility. I thought that I was being autonomous during all those years that I tried to go it alone. In reality, I was just being egotistical and misguided. I accepted—hook, line, and sinker—the idea that society promotes that I was supposed to be independent, that *that* was what it meant to be an adult. I didn't know that being a Christian is "Adulting version 2.0." It's much harder to look after the least of God's people than it is to look after just myself. It's much harder to follow the Way than to let my ego rule. It's much harder to love my enemies than to judge them. But it's much more soul nourishing to do so. It's also better for all creation.

The thing about following Jesus is that it is easier just to accept the invitation and follow him, as hard as that road is, than to reject it. I no longer suffer from ennui or restlessness or depression because I am on the wrong path. I am happy, focused, and energized by my faith. Following Jesus has given me a purpose in life, and that purpose has turned my life around.

I'm still working to get back to that childlike relationship I had with Jesus. My independence asserts itself every once and a while (OK, more than every once in a while!), and always to my detriment. When I start drifting away, things will go awry, letting me know in no uncertain terms that I need to get back to my centre; I need to get back to Jesus. I need to have a little chat with him and listen to what he has to say. Because I don't do this Adulting 2.0 thing alone. He's with me, every step of the way.

> *Michelle Robichaud is an ordained minister of The United Church of Canada and a recent graduate of Atlantic School of Theology. She lives in Eganville, Ontario, with her husband, daughter, two dogs, and one guinea pig.*

4

A Small Season

Heather Ferrier

I pray in the shower. I pray for my congregation as it faces an uncertain future, for the right words to find their way into my mouth while visiting someone who has just lost their husband of 60 years, for people in the news stories I hear while making breakfast, for my family, and for myself, that I might become a little better at following Jesus today than I was yesterday. Well, sometimes I pray all these things. On other days, a tiny face inserts itself between the shower curtain and the tiles while the shampoo is still in my hair, demanding, "Mummy, are you all done your shower yet?" On those mornings, all I can manage is: "Lord, please help me with everything."

I own some wonderful books on spiritual practices, and have even read most of them.

The theory is all there. It's the execution that's lacking. There just never seems to be enough time. I read with envy those accounts of Jesus going into the wilderness to pray, and daydream about what a great Christian I would be if I weren't spending so much time trying to sell my 3-year-old on the merits of putting his pee in the potty. Yet, I know, deep down, that it's the disciple I am day to day, and not the disciple I am on a retreat, that matters. Even if I hadn't known that before, becoming a parent would have revealed it. Now I'm faced each day with a malleable little heart and mind who mimics all that I do and say, sometimes in the most unflattering ways. I want my son to know and follow Jesus, to know the gospel stories, to know that he is loved, and to know how to love others. For that to happen, I have to teach him by example.

So, in this season of my life, I focus on following Jesus in the little things that make up the world of a small child. We hold hands and say grace, act out stories about Jesus with toys, give away outgrown clothes so newer babies can use them, and go for walks and talk about how we should care for nature because it was made by God (which includes taking care of the dog). While running errands, we learn about patience, taking turns, rainbow flags, wheelchair ramps, and to always be kind and say "thank you" to the cashier. We repeat all of these little things, over and over again, in the same way that we re-read this week's favourite bedtime story. These have now become my spiritual practices. There will be time again, someday, for *lectio divina*, the examen, and walking a labyrinth in silence. For now, though, I am following Jesus in the little things that a child can understand, the little things that will impress no one. It's rather humbling, which has been good for me.

The most surprising thing is that I was surprised at all by this change. Throughout scripture, 40 always marks a transformed relationship with God: 40 days and nights of rain, 40 years in the desert, and 40 days in the wilderness. How long is an average human pregnancy? 40 weeks. Parenting books are full of advice on how your body, career, and relationships will change with the arrival of a child, but none that I've read mention faith. Perhaps more theologians need to write parenting books, or more mothers need to become theologians, because how I follow Jesus has been utterly transformed, both by how I seek to teach this little person discipleship, and by how he is teaching me. Jesus once said to his followers, "Whoever welcomes one such child in my name welcomes me" (Matthew 18:5). Now that I've welcomed a child into my life, I'm beginning to understand what he meant.

> *Heather Ferrier is an ordained minister in The United Church of Canada who lives on the South Shore of Nova Scotia with her husband, son, and dog. A graduate of Atlantic School of Theology, Nova Scotia College of Art and Design, and Dalhousie University, she enjoys crafts, folklore, libraries, and Japanese stationary.*

5

Following Jesus to the Lowest Places

Frank Emanuel

I am often reminded of Jesus' teaching that those who would follow him should be prepared to count the cost. My experience of following Jesus is that joining with him in the redemption of the world is a costly adventure. Let me unpack what I mean by "a costly adventure" by telling you some of my story.

We are good at creating slogans in the tradition that I have served the longest, the Vineyard (imagine if Quakers and Pentecostals had a hippie lovechild). Slogans like, "Risk everything for the Kingdom of God" and "Everyone gets to play" capture a sense of what we believe it looks like to follow God as a church. One particular turn of phrase, from our Canadian context, goes like this: "Love, like water, always flows to the lowest place." To me this phrase conveys the sense that following Jesus means going to the places where God's love is needed most. This slogan captured the imagination of the Vineyard congregation that I pastored in Ottawa. Folks in our church looked for opportunities to follow that love wherever it led. Usually, we ended up in places and with people where we did not often see a lot of others like us—evangelical Christians.

At first applying this slogan looked to us like building community with people who were not likely to come out to one of our church services, or to any church service for that matter. We simply enjoyed trying to be an expression of God's love to our new friends. We were careful not to do the typical evangelical thing of being involved with people as subterfuge for making converts. Instead of trying to get our friends into the church, we saw our role as encouragers and examples of the kinds of friends we ourselves would want to have. This was a thrilling time for me. I felt like we were following God into some interesting places. But I would not call what we were doing costly. Still, what we were doing was preparing us for the costly adventure ahead.

One afternoon, one of our worship leaders asked to meet up for dinner. She had been part of our congregation for quite a while and we even walked together through some of life's adversities. I had no idea the reason she had asked me to meet with her that day. Before dinner came, she began to tell me the story of how God had been leading her in a journey of self-discovery and that she had fallen in love with an old friend who was moving to Ontario to be with her. This friend was another woman.

I know that the evangelical church has been a less than hospitable place for queer folk. Previously I had witnessed the harm inflicted on an old flatmate, a gay man who found no safe place in the church, let alone a place that valued him as a gay man. While I have often had queer folk in my life, up until this dinner no one had come out in a church where I pastored. I knew instinctively that this was a terrifying moment for my friend. Trying to be the kind of friend I would like to have, I listened. I even enjoyed her recounting of God's leading in her new relationship. Inside myself, I knew this was going to be costly. I left that meeting with my head aswirl with thoughts. I had never really thought about what I would do in such a situation. I did know that I wanted to do better than what I had seen many evangelical churches do, and I also knew that I needed to see where Jesus was leading.

Our congregation was small, which was a blessing in this situation. My friend continued to lead worship and eventually her partner would also help out at church, even teaching in our meetings. We walked through a few challenges within the congregation, but the sense of community we had was strong enough that the diversity of views did not pose too much of a challenge. Things were considerably harder relating to other churches, even with those in my own tradition. I remember being at one Vineyard leaders' gathering and trembling as I shared how much of a joy it was to have this queer couple leading in our services. Even though that was sometimes uncomfortable in conversations with other pastors, it did not feel that costly yet.

As our congregation wrestled with our feelings around having openly queer folk leading, I too had to wrestle with these same ideas. I remember feeling strongly that God was asking me to not treat any same-sex couple differently than I would any other couple in our church. I am pretty sure God was preparing me for what was to come next. Inevitably the day came when this couple asked if I would marry them.

At that point I had only had a few conversations with other pastors about this possibility and those conversations had not gone well, with a few exceptions. As I tried to navigate my response, I turned to one of those exceptions, my dear friend Brad. At the time, Brad was pastoring a satellite of our congregation near Bancroft, Ontario. Brad's group was an interreligious community, folks who gathered under the premise of wanting to learn how to love God and neighbour better. I loved that Brad was willing to take risks following God, and I knew that his choices had resulted in strained relationships with other pastors in our tradition.

After hearing the story and meeting with the couple and me, Brad offered to co-celebrate and even put the marriage on his register to make it easier for me. I felt that if this was going to be costly then I should gladly bear the cost myself. So, on a lovely October afternoon in 2010, Brad and I performed the wedding. To the best of my knowledge, this was the first same-sex marriage in our Vineyard tradition. The ceremony was a wonderful celebration of love and one of the most Spirit-filled weddings that I have ever had the pleasure of participating in. As someone who served in several traditions where the dominant voices decried same-sex marriage as a godless act, I was overjoyed to find Jesus already ahead of me serving this couple as they gave their lives to each other.

It was several years before leaders in our tradition realized what had occurred. Some were scandalized and worked to push our congregation and me outside of the tradition. Eventually our congregation disbanded. One pastor in our tradition made a point of telling me that they had changed the rules so it would not be easy for me to take on a new pastoral charge. This was despite the fact that I was finishing up a doctorate in theology and currently leading a theological task force for the Canadian Vineyards.

Eventually a new Vineyard congregation started up in our city and my partner Sharon and I became part of that congregation. We were there until it became painfully evident that being an affirming pastor meant that I would never be welcomed to do anything that looked like leading in that church. Meanwhile I was regularly being asked to fill in pulpits in several local churches that were not part of my tradition, some affirming and others not. Since leaving that church, we had the pleasure of helping out with a couple of affirming congregations and experiencing a wonderful freedom that we had never found anywhere else. Freedom like realizing that for the first time, people are not constantly judging us at our church.

This freedom has a cost. Our home tradition continues to push aside congregations that take the affirming path. Recently, we have become part of an affirming Vineyard congregation in Montreal. Our new church was asked to leave the Vineyard tradition over our published statement of belonging and participation. My own ministry credentials remain in question, forcing me to find a new ordaining body to continue my ministry.

I never set out to be an activist, a justice worker, or even a community builder. I set out to follow Jesus. It is in following Jesus that this adventure, this costly adventure, unfolds. I deeply lament the relationships that following Jesus has cost, but even more so I lament the refusal to embrace the implications of our slogans because we think *that* cost is much too high. I mourn the loss of the gifts of those who are rejected and pushed away from evangelical churches, and queer folk are really just the tip of the iceberg here.

My adventure in following Jesus continues. Jesus is still that love that flows to the lowest places and lifts us all up. That kind of Jesus is worth following no matter the cost.

> *Frank Emanuel served with Southminster United Church in Ottawa, and offers workshops on a variety of spiritual topics. He teaches systematic theology at Saint Paul University and the Ottawa School of Theology and Spirituality. Frank also teaches computer programming at Algonquin College and enjoys carpentry.*

6

Sink or Sail

Kimberly Heath

I've been a minister for 21 years, but for many of them, I felt like I was not enough. I kept having an image of being hit by a slow-moving tsunami. This wall of water was headed towards the church I serve, the whole denomination, frankly towards the whole the mainline church in Canada, and there was nothing I could do but watch.

When I entered ministry in the 1990s, the writing was already on the wall. The signs had probably already been there for three decades, but now people were finally starting to notice and talk about it. The church was in rapid decline. In the early years, I naively thought things would be different for me, but more than a decade into my ministry I knew I was fooling myself. My own congregation had gone from two full-time ministers to one (me), and I was doing way more funerals than baptisms or weddings.

While some have adapted their ministry to a sort of spiritual palliative care, that was not my calling. From the beginning I've had a sense of urgency around my ministry. I knew there was no time to waste, but at the same time I felt powerless to do anything that could make any difference.

Blessed are the poor in spirit, for theirs is the Kingdom of heaven.

Maybe Jesus was right, for it was in my powerlessness that I reached out to Jesus. I began to follow Jesus more closely. I have adopted spiritual practices of daily reading from the Bible, memorizing passages of scripture, and prayer. Sometimes prayer looks like journaling and having conversation with God. Sometimes prayer looks like standing in an empty church and bringing to God the people and situations that most need prayer, and sometimes it looks like flipping through a prayer app on my phone.

Following Jesus has also meant connecting regularly with other ministers who have a living faith. I don't do these practices to be more pious, but in order to stay afloat and survive ministry in a challenging time.

I remember a few years back going on a pilgrimage in Nova Scotia. On a pilgrimage you spend a lot of time working through and praying and thinking about your physical and emotional pain. We stayed in churches along the way. I remember one little old Anglican church we stayed in called St. Luke's, in Hubbards, Nova Scotia. It was a beautiful spot with water all around. It had a little basket of small hand-painted rocks for sale (I think they were $10 each). Thinking it was a neat idea and wanting to support this church that had supported us on the way, I started sifting through the rocks when one of them jumped out at me. It was painted blue, with a windsurfer riding the waves.

Do you remember how I was feeling hit by a tsunami? Through this little rock, I felt like

Jesus was telling me there was another way. There was no denying the water and waves, but I felt him saying that *if I filled myself more with God's presence, I would be windsurfing on top of the water instead of drowning under it.* Windsurfers need the wind and the waves to move. They need the wind almost to flow through them so that it can fill that sail in front of them. Windsurfers see the wind and waves in a whole different way than I was seeing them. Wind and waves to a windsurfer are an opportunity, and an adventure! I looked at the image on the rock and I said, Lord, *that's what I want, more of the presence of God.*

The urgency of the waters rising is still with me and I still don't know what the future holds. But reaching out to Jesus has given me fresh hope and reminds me that, on this adventure of ministry, I am not alone.

Great pilot of my onward way, you will not let me drift.
I feel the winds of God today; today my sail I lift.

(from "I Feel the Winds of God Today" by Jessie Adams)

> *Ordained for 24 years, Kimberly has been serving at Wall Street United Church, an active church in the heart of the Thousand Islands in Brockville, Ontario. Kimberly is married with four children and recently completed a Doctor of Ministry degree in preaching.*

7

What It Means For Me To Follow Jesus

Joe Sharpe

I began following Jesus at the age of 22, about 36 years ago. I came "in" as an outsider, not brought up in a church. I had what might be termed a revelation or epiphany, where I realized that Jesus is real. Since that time, following Jesus to me means knowing his character from both the Bible, and from life experiences, both good and bad. I've come to realize that faith is not in my circumstances, but in the truth that Jesus loves me unconditionally. This gives me the ability to treat others with dignity and respect, and I try to focus on that.

For me, to worship Jesus is in how I treat others, including those whom I may not understand, knowing that God loves them unconditionally too. I'll admit that to get to this stage, I had to mature in many ways, and cast off religiosity. One of the most important things that I've been learning is that He does not need to be defended. There is a verse in the Bible that helps me with this: "I have calmed and quieted my soul, like a weaned child with its mother" (Psalm 131:2). This is how I conduct my faith in the midst of all of the "clatter."

I used to feel that I *must* do certain things to be a Christian. When we started raising kids, and I had to back off from "performing." It was very difficult at first, but then I thought about perhaps a believer who may be totally incapacitated by either outside sources or maybe from birth and would therefore unable to "do things" for God. I began to accept my limitations, and chill out!

> *Joe Sharpe is a husband and father of two grown children. He lives in rural Nova Scotia, and teaches guitar for a living. He has been following Jesus since 1986.*

8
The Rock

Penny MacDonald

Upon entering the meeting house, everyone was instructed to pick a rock from a basket on display. We were told it would be an important part of the worship service. Some folks shook their heads No, others casually reached in and grabbed a rock without looking, and then there were people like me who took their time deciding which rock to choose. As a part of the last group, I studied each specimen looking for the right size and shape. Picking up a couple of samples, I pondered which one felt right in my hand. I took my time and found the perfect one for me.

Sitting in the pew, its solid weight felt good as I held it. I admired the smooth spots and was intrigued by the rough edges. The speckles of black and white along with tints of pink gave the rock a freckled look. A few flecks of mica and pyrite flashed as they caught the shine from the overhead lights, making it even more visually appealing. I couldn't resist pulling out my phone and taking a picture of it. As the service progressed, the rock was a comforting presence sitting on my lap, being gently stroked like a cat. Then the moment of truth came. We were instructed to come up front and give our rock to the Saviour.

I hesitated. Give up my rock? No way. I picked it out and had every intention of keeping this beautiful stone. I had already mentally picked out the perfect window ledge to display it at home. It would look great with my other painted rocks and pretty stones. My companion nudged me to get up. Shooting a dirty look in their direction, I slowly rose from my seat and followed the line of people moving to the front. I hung around the back of the line, pretending to be courteous and letting others go before me. Nope—it was more like clinging to my latest possession. The line was getting shorter. *What am I going to do?* I observed others as they casually tossed their stone at the foot of the cross without a thought and others who placed it down lovingly. That is when I felt the Spirit's gentle caress asking, "*Why are you holding on to this burden?*"

What burden? This delightful rock? This need to have it, own it, possess it? How could I forget even briefly that this rock actually belongs to the Saviour and not to me?

Everything that is a part of my life is because of the love Jesus Christ has for me and for everyone. Why couldn't I give back this rock to the creator who is the rock of all salvation? I thought of all the times I prayed to have a heavy weight removed from me ... anger, resentment, fear ... and with relief cast those emotions into Jesus' care. What else was I allowing to weigh me down? How many other weighty objects have I chosen to carry around with me? What else was I holding onto needlessly? What else could I give up to become closer to the Being who loves me more than I can understand?

All these thoughts and questions swirled around in my mind. I mentally laughed at my silliness and was grateful for the simple reminder that our Saviour is always there and always aware. The soothing and healing balm of Gilead flowed over and through me as I happily stepped forward. I placed His rock down at the foot of the cross and whispered, *thank you.*

> *Devoted to learning more about our Saviour Jesus Christ since receiving her first Bible at the age of ten, Penny MacDonald considers it a great blessing to be able to immerse herself in the Lord's word. Growing up, she was able to learn from and attend many different religious denominations and add to her collection of Bibles and the amazing guidance it contains. The amazing beauty of all of God's creation has always been an inspiration to her.*

9

In this world together

Kim McKellar

I take him with me, close
like skin, he tastes the world
as I walk through it, sees it
through my eyes and then
turns the tables, offers me
a glimpse of people changed
by love and compassion,
challenges me to broaden
the reach of my arms and
my mercy and when I do
this, he is with me and when
I fail, he is with me and he is
as alive as I am, for I am
his hands and feet and he
is my heart and soul.

Kim McKellar is a writer and artist living in Ontario. She is the author of two books of poetry, What the Earth Already Knows and Is This Not a Holy Place. She has Master of Pastoral Studies degree from Emmanuel College, Toronto, and lives out her faith primarily through relationship, intentional community and social justice, and the occasional preaching gig.

10

Following Jesus Together

Heather Carlson

"Be subject to one another out of reverence for Christ." (Ephesians 3:21)

My husband and I both met Jesus as children. Later, he was nurtured in conservative Christian traditions, while I was a daughter of two born and bred United Church of Canada ministers. When we met as young adults in the early 1990s, Jason was working retail while I had begun a sociology degree. Jason had just ended a long-term relationship, while I'd had less than a handful of dates. After our first awkward outing together, each of us privately remarked to friends, "It was OK, but it's not like I'd marry him/her."

On the surface, we had little in common, but as we foolishly (or providentially!) continued to see each other, we began to recognize a common desire to follow Jesus's lead in all areas of our life. We were both hungry for studying the Bible, we sought out friends to pray with and for us, we persisted in active church participation, we cherished spiritual mentors, and our correspondence-driven long distance relationship (life before email and cheap long distance calls!) regularly included reflections on sermons, Christian ethics of money and relationships, the church, and all kinds of theology and Christian practice.

When we began to consider marriage, we both felt a bit at sea. His parents were together again after an extended separation and mine were still married, but neither marriage was robust or joy-filled. Was "toughing it out" the goal of Christian marriage? And what would we do with the controversial Biblical passage that was either emblematic of perfection or anathema in our two disparate traditions? *"Wives, be subject to your husbands as you are to the Lord." (Ephesians 5:22).* What sense would we make of that, together?

About that time, I was given a box of old cassette tapes of Everett Fullam. He was an Episcopalian priest who became influential in the 1970s mainline renewal movements. I don't remember how we ended up doing this, but one night Jason and I found ourselves listening to Fullam expound on this verse from Ephesians. Fullam backed up a verse, from verse 22 to verse 21: "*Be subject to one another out of reverence for Christ.*" He lodged marriage in the larger Christian fellowship of the church. As we listened, we were both led to some specific conclusions:

1. Our primary call was to each personally live in joyful obedience to Jesus as our Lord. Disciples first, marriage partners second.

2. Secondly, if we did not agree on something, it didn't mean only one of us was right or got to push to *win*. It meant we did not yet know the will of God. If God joined us together, we'd have to trust that he would not lead us in separate directions.

3. Jesus wanted our marriage not only to survive, but thrive. We'd do the work necessary to be *happily* married.

Nine months into marriage, the cancer Jason's Mom had battled returned and left her incapacitated. When the hospital team laid out the options, we were looking at either a long-term care placement two hours away, or coming up with a family plan to cover 24/7 care. Both options seemed daunting and unpalatable, and we couldn't agree about what was best. A few weeks later when the decision had to be made, Jason and I found ourselves readily agreeing to move in with his folks to cover the care needed. Astonished at the change in ourselves and one another, we recognized Jesus had been at work in us and in our marriage! He kept us on the same page and grew our attitudes and actions. We look back on that challenging final year with his Mom as a treasured opportunity.

Another example of following Jesus in our marriage came a number of years later during a season of strains that were draining our energy and increasing our discontent. Our eleventh wedding anniversary was marked more by disconnection than delight, and we realized we'd lost that sense of being a team. Things didn't improve all at once, but change began when Jason and I were independently brought back to principle #1 above. Jesus can't be Lord of our marriage if one or both of us push him out of top spot personally. And Jesus can't mend and grow our marriage if we aren't consistently listening and following his directions.

Following Jesus in that season of life meant some practical things like getting help from counselors, kick-starting regular prayer, fleeing temptations, finding healthy marriage mentors, and lots of day-to-day acts of confession and kindness. As we sought to follow Jesus' way of self-giving love, we began to recognize his presence at work in re-establishing marital unity and joy.

We recently celebrated our 25th wedding anniversary. Our Facebook announcement said "*25 years trusting God to lead us together, not *apart. 25 years of doing the work to be happily married, not just legally entangled."*

We have faced a lot of decisions, dilemmas, and challenges in those years. We find ourselves recounting those foundational underpinnings for marriage more frequently as time passes. They are the three-way vows we made in our youth, and the way we continue to follow Jesus as he grows and shapes us and our marriage.

> *Heather Carlson lives in Drumheller, Alberta, with her husband Jason and their two teens. After twenty years of ministry leadership in The United Church of Canada, Heather now works in Community Development with the municipality. She enjoys prayer, deep questions, abundant laughter, theatre, Biblical study, making soup, hiking, reading, and family time.*

11

Jesus: Baggage, Blame, and Bathwater

Jennifer Swanson

For a long time, when asked what I did for work, I would hesitate and make that ever-so-split decision as to whether or not I should reveal that I am a member of the cloth. Not because I was embarrassed, or because I don't think it's a worthy calling (it is, after all, my third career path and one I had resisted for some time before acquiescing), but because if revealed that fact, it invariably involved a change in behaviour on the part of the other person. Frankly, when that happened, it all felt too much like work.

At secular social gatherings, or networking events for my other work, or when new neighbours move in, I sometimes just didn't want to feel The Shift: the slight stiffening, the dawning realization, the "oh really?" polite yet awkward response, followed by an unsolicited explanation of what brand of Christianity the person was raised in, or worse—why they are too busy to attend anymore. It was as though I had suddenly thrown up four intricately carved walls and a little velvet curtain and put out my confessional sign saying the preacher was "in."

I think I prefer the French, who find it exceedingly rude even to ask what one's profession is, and instead ask what you are passionate about or what captivates you or what keeps you interested in life. That is a far more engaging conversation most of the time and dips into the same depths of humanity I am captivated by.

And yet I find myself tired; hair-shirt ripping, knees to the river-bank, table-flipping-over tired of Jesus being co-opted by one particular brand that in most ways resembles nothing about how I experience him and his life story. Let's face it, Jesus comes with a whole lot of baggage these days. The unfortunate way in which his message has often been interpreted has in several cases caused irreparable damage and tragedy, and it rightly deserves the blame. If I didn't know Jesus from Adam, I too would not bother.

So why do I? This is a question much of my very anti-religious family of origin cannot figure out the answer to.

Because there is just something about the guy.

If you go to the Bible, which admittedly is a collection of human interpretation, and explore the context of the gospel stories, and learn about what was going on in and around when the oral stories were captured in print, there is still compelling news there. Jesus was social. He needed people. He worked with all kinds of people and didn't seem to be very picky about who was "in" or not. He had a strong bent for social justice. He followed the rules and norms sometimes, when it made sense to his mission, and he didn't go on about his rights or what he deserved to be doing or getting. Instead, he was very much about the collective and especially about the ones for whom life was especially hard. And he was pretty weird.

In a good way.

I suspect if Jesus was plunked into any Grade 5 classroom today he'd have one heckuva time because he did not conform. He wasn't out to be popular. His message wasn't sexy or avant-garde or even entertaining. He came with peace and love on the tongue and made it happen by healing and teaching and talking and drinking and eating and showing his new vision to whomever he was with.

I don't think he was perfect. I don't want to whitewash his humanity because I think it dilutes the divine in him. I think that's the bathwater that has filled up the mythology around him through poor interpretation and the quest for control that has clouded everything. And yet this baby is worth saving, not throwing out with that bathwater.

For those who can see past the hurts and missteps of religion; for those who don't claim to know everything there is to know but are instead fiercely and gently open to wonder; for those curious enough to be vulnerable and not afraid of dissolving into a puddle of uncertainty when the gospel yet again upends "the way it is" and allows glimpses into new realms; well . . . *there is nothing like it.*

That's the Jesus I know, and the one I continue to encounter, seek out and learn from. That's the one who has me mesmerized and the one whose message permeates my life and my work. All my work. Even my seemingly secular career stuff that I still do part time.

And if you ask me at a BBQ what I do for living, I might sigh just a little, and with a slight smile, I might answer, "I'm in sales," which would not be entirely inaccurate.

> *Jenn Swanson is an ordained minister in The United Church of Canada and came to this calling later in life. She began in health care and then teaching college and career coaching while raising a family. Then "God got her." She finally said yes and studied at the Vancouver*

School of Theology. She graduated and was ordained in 2014. Jenn currently serves part time in a thriving community of faith in Port Moody, British Columbia, and still teaches and coaches in the career realm on YouTube when not puttering in the garden or making a delicious mess in the kitchen. Jenn lives with her husband Scott and hangs out with their four grown children and one brilliant grandson whenever possible.

12

Down in the Valley with Jesus

Susan Girard

I have followed Jesus—or should I say, Jesus has watched out for me, guided me, cared for me, renewed me, and given me wisdom—since I was eighteen years old. I have no doubt that I have been loved and cherished by Him all my life, even before I was born, but I only consciously chose to be in a relationship with Him since I was eighteen. I am sure life got better for both of us at that juncture.

It has been quite the journey; never a dull moment through life's many mountaintop and valley experiences, and everything in between. Popeye's secret power was spinach. Mine is prayer to the One who shared our human vulnerabilities and walked amongst us and is accessible to us 24 hours a day, seven days a week through the Holy Spirit.

Little did I know of the spiritual challenge ahead of me when I received a phone call from my gynecologist informing me that my endometrial biopsy revealed I had grade two cancer. She explained that with grade one, the cancer cells divide at about the same rate as our other cells; grade three is an aggressive cancer; and grade two is somewhere in between. I would be scheduled for a hysterectomy within six weeks.

My world stopped. All I could do was pray in a state of shock until my husband got home and I was given the courage and strength to tell him. His first wife had died of cancer, as did one of his daughters. In spite of this traumatic history, we were both remarkably hopeful.

Following another doctor's appointment at the Cancer Center, I was sent for a CT scan of my chest, abdomen, and pelvis. One week after my cancer diagnosis, my gynecologist phoned me again informing me that, as a consequence of having cancer, my body was in an inflammatory state resulting in blood clots in my lungs. I was to go to emergency immediately.

I was not happy. Let me rephrase that. I was angry, afraid, and did not want anything to do with hospitals or doctors. But I found myself sitting in emergency and giving my information to the nurse at the desk. All I could do was pray. After more blood tests and assorted other tests, I was sent home with needles containing blood thinner that I was to inject myself with daily, at the same time each day and in the folds of fat around my waist.

Fortunately, finding folds of fat was not a problem. The bigger issue was injecting myself.

Let me explain. I never look when I get an injection. That strategy was not going to work if I was going to successfully give myself a daily injection. My life depended upon it.

Sitting there in the hospital, I prayed silently. By the time I left the hospital, needles and small sharps container in hand, I had resolved that if young children can learn to inject themselves with insulin, then I could inject myself. After two weeks of injections that went very well, and that resulted in numerous bruises all over my stomach, I was running out of room and wondering if there was some other spot on my body where I could give myself injections. The phone rang, and a very kind nurse practitioner from the blood clinic introduced himself and asked me if I wanted to continue with the injections or change to a tablet.

I laughed. When I finally stopped laughing, he said that believe it or not many people want to continue with the injections. "That would not be me!" I said, very relieved.

The date of my surgery arrived. I was afraid. No one would know the progression of the cancer until after the surgery and the pathology report. Again, I received strength and courage from prayer. I was so afraid that I could not sense the presence of God. All I could do was trust. I knew people were praying for me. I was walking on water.

Unstable on my feet because of the pre-operative drugs I had received, I held a nurse's arm as we walked to the operating room. As I laid down on the operating table, I surrendered again to Jesus, giving Him all of me, body and soul. I was completely powerless. I did not know why I got cancer or why I got blood clots. I never had major surgery before. So many things were out of my control. No matter the outcome, I knew I was not alone.

I woke in the recovery room, disoriented and not knowing if I had had the surgery. I had lost all sense of time and place. A nurse informed me the surgery was over. As I laid my head down to sleep, all I could hear were loud beeps and people running towards me telling me to breathe deeply. This scene repeated itself many times until the anesthetic wore off. Apparently, my breathing became dangerously slow and shallow when I fell asleep, a common occurrence after surgery. I had to spend a night in the hospital and was discharged the next day.

I was told someone would phone me with

the results of the pathology report in about ten days. That was a truly challenging time for me. The surgeon had informed me she had removed more suspicious tissue than expected. If the cancer had spread, I wondered if it had spread throughout my body. Along with everyone else, I would have to wait for the pathology report. During this uncertain time, my mind often travelled to thoughts of dying and death, and then I would become hopeful again that all would be well.

Prayer sustained me. That fact cannot be overstated.

I came to realize that if my path was about becoming palliative and dying, I would be given the grace to walk that path. I trusted that wisdom. I trusted Jesus was with me and would never leave me. I was still afraid and paradoxically more peaceful. I knew this cancer was not some kind of divine punishment. I realized that I got cancer because I am human and live in a deeply wounded world. Some human beings get cancer, and some human beings that get cancer die. I wanted to live. Whatever the outcome, I knew I was not alone.

I felt like I was falling into the arms of God, over and over, and over again. I poured all my fears and hopes, all my thoughts and ruminations into prayer, knowing that the One who received them shared my human vulnerabilities and fears.

About ten days later, a doctor from the Cancer Centre phoned and told me my report had arrived and that I had had stage 1b endometrial cancer. She explained if I had three brachytherapies (internal radiation treatments lasting about ten minutes each), the chances of not getting endometrial cancer again were close to 90%. I followed all medical advice, had the three brachytherapies, and am now on my way to living a healthy life once again. God did not give me cancer. However, I trust that God will use that experience for my good and the good of others.

Why do I follow Jesus?

Jesus knows me better than I know myself.

He is my soul friend, the God in whom I can trust, who always has my back and my best interests at heart. Compassionate, merciful, wise and kind, the source of my life, closer to me than my own breath. I cannot comprehend the depth of love God has for me, always forgiving. I can pour out my heart and soul to God without fear. Jesus is my source and my destination, the God on whom my whole life depends, today and all days. What an adventure!

> *Susan Girard is a life-long follower of Jesus, minister, life-long learner, wife, mom, step-mom, grandmother, great-grandmother, and companion of two furry well-loved poochies.*

13

Lead. Follow. Leave.

Deborah Ambridge Fisher

I follow Jesus because on Sunday, April 8, 2012, Easter Sunday, I sat sobbing in church as it hit me, really hit me, that Jesus loves me. I had never really allowed myself to think that before. I had kept Jesus at arm's length because deep in my heart I did not believe I was worthy of such incredible love and sacrifice. I had gone to church my entire life, but I had never been told I was loveable. All I knew was that I needed to be *more*, or *better*. I could be me, of course, just "not like that."

That Easter Sunday all that was swept away in a flood of tears as I realized that I was deeply and unconditionally loved. I was *enough*. I always had been and I always would be. *Enough*.

I often tease the minister who was in the pulpit that day that it was something he said that opened my heart and mind, but I just have no idea what it was. I have a copy of his sermon and I take it out every few years to see if I can pinpoint exactly what sentence or phrase cracked my soul open that day . . . but I always know the effort is futile. It was the Spirit, having had enough of gentle nudging I suppose, and she decided that day to bodycheck me onto the path I was meant to follow. Following Jesus has been really hard though. Just when I think I have figured out the path I am on, the Spirit hipchecks me onto the next one . . . and I am never ready.

I hate camping. I'm terrible at it. I need to buy new shoes, clothing, and gear . . . and there is never a map. I have no desire to blaze a trail and I have no idea how to pitch a tent, start a fire, or forage for food. Starting anything over again is my least favourite thing to do. Honestly, I hate new paths and sometimes, sometimes I want to get off the path altogether. I want to leave my leaky tent and check into a hotel that has everything I need without me having to work for it.

Following Jesus has been hard because it has taken me to painful places where I was asked to act as witness to grief and death, and then I had no power to alleviate it. I try to love everyone I meet, I really do, even when they very clearly do not love me. I have tried to show kindness in the face of cruelty, only to fail and wonder if I am really cut out for this. Jesus can be really hard to follow because I don't always like the people I have to walk with, and sometimes I just want to stop.

But I am not stopping.

Following Jesus is hard sometimes, sure, but it is also the best adventure I have ever been on and I know I won't stop. Being a follower of Jesus has taken me on a journey I would never have thought possible. Just when I think the path is too hard, things happen that could only have happened to me on that path. Holding the hand of someone as they take their final breath, and giving thanks that you made it on time to pray with them and their loved ones. Struggling to hold a wiggly baby wrapped in satin and trying not to drop them in the baptismal font as I preside over the most sacred of sacraments. Being the first person to introduce a newly married couple. Following Jesus means being invited into the best and worst parts of people's lives and then leaving, always feeling immense gratitude.

And the people! Okay, there are some people I really wish I could leave behind me, that's true. But there are so many more people out there who shone so brightly I don't even need to look all that hard before I find God in them. There are people who have taught me, laughed with me, cried with me, and picked me up when I have fallen.

There are also people who insist on making me sing but that is a story for another time.

Those people are the best part of following Jesus . . . and I know I am being led away from them. Starting over is my least favourite thing but I know I am about to step off this path, and this time there isn't a trail to follow. I admit that

I am a bit afraid this time because I am leaving a place of comfort and heading off into . . . well, God knows what. Following Jesus means going where I am sent, rather than staying where I am comfortable. Whether I like it or not.

December 24, 2020 was the beginning of the end of my current journey. I just didn't know it then. In a counselling session my therapist asked me if I had ever heard of the business model, "Lead. Follow. Leave." She explained that leaders need to know when to lead and when to follow, obviously. But the trick, she said, is to know when to leave. I wrote those three words and taped them to the wall next to my impromptu, COVID-necessitated desk. I would look at those words almost daily for the next four months. I knew what God was trying to tell me in those three words. I just wasn't prepared to admit it.

For me, following Jesus also means knowing when it is time to leave the path I thought I was meant to follow. It means giving up what I know and moving into the unknowable. It means trusting the Spirit when she bodychecks me onto a newer, hidden path that I am expected to walk alone . . . at least for the time being. I admit that I am frustrated. The shoes I just bought were not made for this new path and there are no clear places to make camp. Following Jesus is pretty scary sometimes and that hotel is looking really tempting.

> *Deborah Ambridge Fisher is partner to John and mummy to Emilia. She has a greyhound who is the best thing ever (after John and Emilia of course).*

14

Pews for Sale

Heather Fletcher

A *Ramble*

Jesus moved in on a Tuesday. I had spoken to my partner a few nights earlier, yearning for a giant wooden cross for our dining room table.

"We can't!" he laughs. "Everyone will think we're trying to convert them."

"It's not that," I giggle. "It's for glory and thanks."

Something must have cooked up in his brain, as he returned home a few days later from a country auction with a two-foot-four-inch statue of Jesus and four icons of our Lord and Mother Mary.

We placed "Statue Jesus" under the windowsill. He's the perfect height to give our dog's bum a good scratch. He stands above our heating vent, which gives ghostly life to the green scapular hung around his hand. I come visit Him when the screens and digital demands of working-from-home get too much. Jesus holds up His hands. "Everybody just relax," He says. Even in a pandemic, He is still the perfect Prince of Peace. I carefully hold the scapular and recite the prayer etched on the back. "*Coeur Immaculé de Marie, priez pour nous maintenant et à l'heure de notre mort,*" it reads. Immaculate Heart of Mary, pray for us now and at the hour of our death.

Ruins

Just outside our living room window, we can see the gravel pit that was once home to Ontario Street Baptist Church. It has been a vacant lot for a couple of years, and I often think how the house behind must miss its shadow. The church was sold and demolished for an insurance building that, ironically, couldn't build its cornerstone during a pandemic after all. Broken bones of church columns and stone fixtures remain piled in an adjacent parking lot. The neighbourhood is left to sit with this decision. I wonder if anyone else is thinking what I'm thinking: *And what of my Father's house?*

It's Christmas Eve 2019 and I am teary-eyed. I hold my Mom's hand; she has stepped down from the pulpit to sit with me and sing a carol. Will anyone remember these hymns? This candlelight? When I am a mother, where will I take my child to sing carols?

Fall 2020 arrives and the rain hits our boots as the bells of St. James Church play us into the Slow Food Market. We buy a chicken, croissants, and red beets. The same nostalgic sound of heartbreak rips through my eardrums as I wonder who is playing the bells today. Will these sounds still play us into worship in 20 years? Here we are in Babylon, and everything is uncertain. There are wisps of familiarity because we get to journey together, but the only certainty is the uncertainty. The despair of Asaph is as relevant today as it was then, as if he's just updated his Facebook status:

"We do not see our emblems; there is no longer any prophet, and there is no one among us who knows how long" (Psalm 74:9).

Will we ever get to return, will we ever get to rebuild the Lord's house?

I drive from this town to that town and some churches are closing up shop. "Pews for sale," say the signs. We pull over, compelled to fit one into our vehicle. "We only have circular ones," they say. I wince at the idea of cutting them, like snapping a spine in two. *Lord, if only I could buy them all.* I spend hours on real estate websites looking for churches to buy, wanting to save them from demolition. Here I am a Holy Hoarder trying to gather every piece of the physical church I possibly can. I think of the sprawl and mourn for the beauty. Do we really need more condos? Can we not keep just one sacred sanctuary?

Oh Lord, I know you are in Everything
but sometimes I need
sanctuary.

Repentance

As the daughter of two ministers of The United Church of Canada who served four pastoral charges, I have borne witness to many church funerals. In 2019, the National Trust for Canada estimated that close to 9000 churches would close in the next few years. I brace myself for the probability that the pandemic will accelerate this decline. Instead of 20 years, do we now have two? What does this new timeline mean for us?

In 2018, when my Dad was on life support, I had the honour of attending a workshop in his place, which was put on by the London-area United Church conference. As I sat with the parallels and complexities of trying to preserve the life of those we love (my Dad, our church), a breath of fresh air whooshed in from one of the conference presenters. Instead of denying the church's death, and hurriedly scrambling to resuscitate, how might we lead the church gracefully into palliative care?

Ah yes, there it is.

Oh gosh, here we go.
Acceptance of death!
Death... with dignity!

Now I'm home again with two-foot-four-inch Statue Jesus. His stance is the same, His reflection unchanged. He is constant. It's communion Sunday and I have logged onto virtual church. I take a piece of bread from our cupboard. It is stale and difficult to break. We use it later for breadcrumbs on pasta. Jesus speaks from across the centuries, through Scripture. *"This is my body, which is given for you. Do this in remembrance of me"* (Luke 22:19). I realize in hindsight that this particular breaking of stale bread is even more symbolic.

He who came with radical love, to break the stale,
tear the veil,
overturn the tables of the world that was,
see the forgotten,
to say,
"Look, here.

Love is needed here."

The church has been kind to me and I am grateful for it. This is where I learn and where I come to listen. It is where I know Majesty. Not everyone has had this experience. The divisions and differences are real.

Is deconstruction part of God's plan?

Is demolition necessary to rebuild a new framework?

Is death part of the Church's . . . life?

We believe in the resurrection, but to have the resurrection we must have death. This thought of repentance is inviting.

Ultimately, what should we let die?

And what should we rebuild?

Maybe, just maybe, Jesus is calling us beyond the sanctuary. Maybe we're missing the mark.

Reverence

Jesus takes my hand, and pulls me up to the mountaintop. We have hiked for hours and were it not for His hand, I would have given up miles ago to eat granola bars and cheese sandwiches. I breathe in the landscape before us. "I have given you all this," He speaks. "What have you done with it?"

It's a sobering moment of stewardship—a call to experience, a call to evolve. He has asked my greatest fear and provided my largest inspiration.

I chew on veneration.
Reading,
praying,
fasting,
deconstructing.

I research the green scapular. One of its benefits is the assurance of a happy death. I begin a month of reading Luke, craving time with Jesus as He journeys to the cross. On day one, as Mary is contemplating both her own and Elizabeth's miracle pregnancies, I am brought both to tears and to my knees at the shattering simplicity of the gospel: *"For nothing will be impossible with God"* (Luke 1:37). This powerful promise reverberates through the rest of Luke, and through my daily doubts.

I continue on. Behind every miracle is compassion. Each teaching is rooted in fairness and unconditional love. Every outburst is a call to justice. I follow Jesus because he eloquently does what I wish I could do every time I'm in a boardroom: to call out the truth, no matter how many turn against you for it. We are encouraged to leave physical possessions, to walk in faithful confidence knowing that not only our needs will be provided for, but that we will be led to where we need to be. This includes the church.

For nothing will be impossible with God.
Nothing.

My longing for the physical church is a scramble to preserve every little bit I can. I want to save the institution because I'm fearful the knowledge won't be passed on without its presence. But His plans are greater than mine.

I realize I can't do the saving. I can't buy all the pews. They've already been purchased.

The Spirit is going to change things.
The Spirit will keep moving
with or without bricks and mortar.
In the desert, in the wilderness,
the Spirit will never die.

I will still attend every fundraising dance, and dance my little feet off until the last brick stands. I will still purchase tickets to pork or beef dinners even though I'm pescatarian, and I will savour the mashed potatoes and side salad because I love the church *that* much. And I will seek Jesus with all of my heart, because I believe in His transformative power of life-giving change.

Great Pillar of Fire,
Voice of Esther,
Life-giver to Elizabeth, Hannah and Lazarus,
Holy One.
Let us revere and rally to the reality of the resurrection.
Forgive me for confining You to four walls.

With a love for short stories and poetry, Heather Fletcher's passion projects are writing about grief and the Divine's hand through life-death-life narratives. Heather is the daughter of Reverends Mary and Terry Fletcher (Terry passed away in June 2018). She now lives in St Marys, Ontario with her partner and a spectacular kangaroo of a dog.

15

Why I Follow Jesus Today

William N. Drysdale

I began ministry some 30 years ago, although I did not realize what I was doing. Since that time, I have been supported by many friends who made my ministry possible. As a result of their support, I have been in part-time ministry since 2005 as a Designated Lay Minister. The most wonderful part of all of this is that it has been rewarding, fulfilling, and challenging. I would not wish to be anywhere else in my journey.

I believe it was in March 1988. After 14 months in a 12-step recovery program, I found myself struggling with many new thoughts and ideas. I just could not seem to get myself around "a power greater than me." To say that I was self-centered would be an understatement. In my early years, I had never been fully aware of any presence of any kind but me. It seemed the harder I worked at it, the harder it got.

I remember someone saying to me, "Fake it until you make it." There was no way I was going to do that, because my whole life was a lie. I would not take responsibility for anything I did in my life. A friend of mine dropped by to see if I was OK. I didn't want to talk to anyone. Then my friend said something that caught me off guard. They said, "I prayed to Jesus about you last night." My first thought was, *who asked you to pray for me?* Imagine someone not open to having someone pray for them! Yet that is exactly who I was at that time. I can't really tell you what happened after that, but the thought of someone praying to Jesus *for me* never left my mind.

It wasn't long after that when I had to get honest with myself. On one of my visits to my parents' home, while I was walking in nature, I offered a simple prayer to God: *God what do you want me to do?* On that day I had a thought: *You will be a fisher of men.*

I had no idea what that meant, so I asked others. Often they would say, "You don't want to do that," or, "You are too old to begin such a journey." Nobody was willing to tell me what I didn't want to do. I had done a thorough self-examination and asked God for forgiveness. The thing that was truly amazing is that forgiveness was not able to come until I could forgive myself. It was truly amazing for on that day, at that moment, I knew for the first time in my life that God cared about me. I was forgiven that day and a new world opened to me.

In 1992, I was remarried and my partner, Pat, and I chose The United Church of Canada as our church home. This in itself was another kind of story because I was Anglican at the time. But my partner didn't like the Anglican Church's structure. I was invited to sing at a friend's wedding at a United Church. After the wedding, Pat said to me, "now, I would get married in this church." When I reflect back on moments such as this, it seems to me that this journey was not so much my decision, but the decisions of many people.

The minister at that wedding was new, young, and open, and we spent much time in conversation. When I shared with him my concerns about answers I could not seem to find, he encouraged me to continue my search with him. After a year or so of meeting every other week, he suggested I should take a Diploma Program in Theology and Ministry at Atlantic School of Theology. He told me there were only three seats left in the course. I asked if he would contact AST for me, and he agreed. The next day he called to say that there were only two spots left, because I was registered for that third opening. I was so excited! Things were beginning to take on a completely new meaning, not just for myself but also for Pat. It was a three-year program of part-time studies at home and on campus. It was an amazing journey that often gave me more questions than answers. I found myself deep in discussion about life, people, and God. I was searching, discerning, and growing at last in my understanding of "a power greater than myself."

There were many people who suggested I didn't know what I was doing. Yet at the same time, all of this was giving new purpose to my life. It was so exciting just to listen and learn. After completing the program, I wanted more. I went through a discernment process and realized that I might be able to enter the Lay Ministry Program. Throughout all of this, I kept hanging on to the memory that someone had prayed for me to Jesus. I felt like Jesus heard those prayers.

My discernment to serve in ministry hit a few speed bumps. At one point, it seemed that what I had hoped for was not going to happen. I was going to have to change educational paths again because the program I wanted to follow was discontinued. Although many before me had followed that other path, which led through university, this felt impossible. My previous schooling was limited and I had never done well as a learner. About eight years later, the

Lay Ministry Program became available again and I was accepted. I believed in my heart that if God wanted me in ministry, I would be in ministry. Those were the very words I told a group of ministers when I was interviewed as a ministry student. They informed me that many people felt the same way and were not in ministry. But I persisted.

After nearly 10 years, I was finally granted entry into the Lay Ministry Program and was to off to school at McGill University. I was absolutely in shock. I didn't think I was wise enough to attend. I worried terribly. At the very first session in Montreal, the instructor introduced herself. She said, "Some of you here think you cannot learn. But I want you to know that I have been teaching for many years. We are going to teach to your strength and not your weakness."

What I was told on that day in 2005 totally changed my thinking. Since that time, I have never forgotten any of those learning sessions. They are engraved on my mind and have helped to make me follow Jesus even more. It has enriched my faith and my ability to speak to those who struggle because they may not think like others. It has helped me to appreciate those who teach in a way that opens doors that seem to be closed. It also allows me to be grateful for all those who have helped to prepare the way for my ministry. I cannot ask for any more than that.

I have been blessed in serving the church and its people. I have not always had the support of everyone, but I have always offered myself to everyone. One of the blessings I have is my own story. I recall times of interviewing others who wanted to offer their ministry to the church. One time, a minister said, "When I did my interview, there were those who gave me a hard time. So I believe it's my job to give others a hard time!" But I think we should be more open minded, open to the Spirit, and open to each other. It is a great responsibility to select future ministers. I want to hear and respect the passion they have to serve others.

Today, I am full of gratitude. I have celebrated 34 years of sobriety and 16 years in ministry. I take it one day at a time. Maybe none of this would be possible without someone praying to Jesus for me more than 30 years ago.

> *William Drysdale is the oldest of seven siblings born in Halifax, Nova Scotia. He served briefly in the Canadian Army and now serves as a Designated Lay Minister with three United Churches in rural Nova Scotia.*

16

Walking with the Followers of Jesus, 1968-1990

Tadashi (Tad) Mitsui

For me, following Jesus means to join the company of his followers. I cannot do it alone. I am not brave. I witnessed the martyrdom of those who followed Jesus as they fought for justice in Palestine and South Africa. But I am like the Roman centurion who watched Jesus die on the cross from a safe distance and said, *"This man was innocent."*

The people I accompanied were following Jesus in varied ways. Some were agnostics, humanists, Christians, or Muslims. Regardless of different labels, they were moved by the same Spirit. Like the centurion who might have been a pagan, they reached the same conclusion as Jesus' followers. They gave them-selves entirely to the cause of justice, love, and peace . . . salaam . . . shalom. When a theological college awarded me an honorary degree, I did not feel worthy. I accepted it to celebrate those followers of Jesus I had known, and I named them in my acceptance speech. I am a witness to those who paid the ultimate cost of discipleship.

People must wonder if I am a reckless adventurer seeking excitement by being involved in the struggles of Palestinians and South Africans. It was not like that. I took the job that came my way, and realized the price of the choices I had unwittingly made. Nevertheless, I wanted to run away every time I came face to face with harsh reality, like Peter did.

We went to Africa because, after eleven years in my first pastoral charge, I wanted change. I applied for an overseas posting with The United Church of Canada. Norman McKenzie, the personnel officer of the Division of World Outreach, asked me, "Africa or Asia?" I said, "Africa." He asked, "Lesotho?" I had never heard of such a country, but I said, "Yes." That's how I stumbled into the struggle against apartheid in South Africa in 1968. Was I seeking an adventure? No.

Lesotho is a tiny landlocked mountain kingdom surrounded by South Africa. The Paris Missionary Society of French Reformed Churches asked The United Church of Canada to recruit an English-speaking person with a graduate degree in theology. After a few months of orientation in Paris, we went to Lesotho where I met extraordinary colleagues and students. Some of their names you may recognize and others not, but each of them were equally committed to the struggle for justice. Desmond Tutu was my colleague in theology at the University of Botswana, Lesotho, and Swaziland. John Osmers was the chaplain of the Student Christian Movement. Another colleague, Anthony Gann, was already prohibited to enter South Africa. The university had many South African students who were activists in the Black Consciousness Movement created by Steve Biko. They came to Lesotho to avoid racially segregated university education. One was Njabulo Ndebele, who later became president of the University of Cape Town. Another was Jama Mbeki, a brother of the second president of free South Africa, Thabo Mbeki. Jama simply disappeared from the campus in 1971. To this day, nobody knows what happened to him.

In January 1971, I was detained at the Detention Centre in Johannesburg Airport while returning from a conference in Tanzania. Thereafter, I was expelled and prohibited further entry into the Republic of South Africa. At the time, I had no idea why it happened to me. I was not looking for trouble. I had not done or said anything subversive. I stayed in Lesotho for five more years, unable to leave the land-locked country. Dentists were available only in South Africa. I had to ask someone to take my car into South Africa for service. To leave the country, I had to fly via a South African airport where I was escorted by Canadian embassy staff. It became impossible to send my daughter to an English language secondary school outside of the country. We had to leave Southern Africa.

I took up a position in the World University Service (WUS) international headquarters in Switzerland. It enabled me to continue working with the same people in Southern Africa. I administered funds to support the work of those who were engaged in the struggle for the freedom in South Africa. I always flew to Lesotho to meet with my partners from South Africa as I was not allowed to travel there.

I came safely home while others stayed to pay a price. Many died in the struggle. In 1976, Mapetla Mohapi was found dead in a prison cell in King Williams Town. He was probably killed while being tortured. Police were trying to find the names of overseas financial supporters of the Black Consciousness Movement (BCM). One of them was the World University Service, my later employer. Mohapi was the treasurer of the BCM. His wife, Nohle, wrote to me to say that it was the worst possible time for her. Their first child had just been born and they just had a roof repaired. Griffith Mxenge, who was a lawyer for the BCM, was found shot dead on the street a few months after he and I had a meeting in Lesotho to discuss administrative matters. A year after Mohapi's death, Steve Biko was beaten to death in the same prison. The whole world knows what happened to Steve Biko. But there was no real difference between those who lived or died. Following Jesus means one accepts the risk, the roll of the dice.

Two of my friends, John Osmers and Michael Lapsley, both Anglican chaplains, were nearly killed by parcel bombs. They lost a few limbs but survived. Abram Tiro was blown to bits in exile in Gaborone, Botswana, with a parcel bomb. The bombs were sent from Geneva, most likely by a person who I had thought to be my good friend. He pretended to be a refugee. Sometimes following Jesus means you may run into Judas.

While still in Lesotho, I asked the Canadian

Embassy in South Africa to discover the reason for my detention and expulsion. It took several years. Initially, the Canadian Embassy in Cape Town dismissed my request for inquiry. This was how their letter began, "As a Canadian of non-European origin, etc., etc." It sounded as though I did something wrong and Canada had two-tier citizenship. There was a strong protest from The United Church of Canada, spearheaded by Garth Legge, General Secretary of World Outreach, and by my home Conference of British Columbia. Mitchell Sharp, the Canadian Minister for External Affairs, finally apologized and informed me that it seemed the South African authorities saw me as undesirable because of the kind of colleagues and friends I had. I didn't choose them; they were there when I got there. Following Jesus can place you among the outcasts.

I also met brave people in Palestine when I worked for the Canadian Council of Churches from 1979 to 1990. Part of my job was to represent Canadian churches that supported the Middle East Council of Churches. Also, for three months in 2003, I joined the Ecumenical Accompaniment Program of the World Council of Churches and lived in the West Bank village of Jayyous. One day, some farmers were prevented from going to their fields by a barricade and curfew, leading to a tense encounter between them and Israeli soldiers. Many young Israeli peace activists and my co-workers in the Accompaniment Program rushed to be with the farmers to provide them safe space. There was tear gas shot into the crowd. Where was I? I ran away to wash my eyes with a raw onion—an antidote for tear gas. I had to face the fact that I was not brave. Following Jesus teaches you humility.

I met many brave Christian Palestinians in the Gaza Strip and West Bank, including Constantine Dabbagh, Doris Saleh, and Albert Nursy. They were the members of the Refugee Service Committee of the Council of Churches. Another was Emil Aghaby, a businessman who volunteered to administer the Middle East

Council of Churches' program in the refugee camps in Lebanon. He was later found shot dead on the road. They were all well-educated, middle-class Palestinians. By the 1980s, most middle-class Palestinian Christians had left for safer living conditions in other countries, and their numbers dropped from 26% to 5% of the total Palestinian population in the Holy Land. But my colleagues stayed behind to help those who could not migrate. Many traced their ancestry to the original Christians, the original followers of Jesus.

Saying "Yes" to Lesotho changed my life. By chance, it set me on the road to South Africa and to Palestine. And on the road to Emmaus. The encounters on that path taught me many lessons. Those with whom I walked paid a heavy price. I am a witness for them.

> *Tadashi (Tad) Mitsui was born in Japan and studied at Tokyo Union Theological Seminary and Union College at the University of British Columbia, and received an honorary degree*

from United Theological College at McGill University. An ordained minister of The United Church of Canada, he served local churches, as Overseas Personnel, as a lecturer in theology, and for organizations such as the World University Service and the Canadian Council of Churches.

17

Al's having a baby!

Allan David Smith-Reeve

Over and over again, the liberating, transforming, power of Jesus saves me from my self-absorption and calls me to serve. The day that service came alive was June 9, 1988—the day my daughter was born. On that day, Alana Sarah transformed me into a father. She arrived in this world with an ancient and perfect soul. As my purpose as a man deepened into fatherhood, my calling to serve the people of my city—finally—also took shape. The two were intertwined.

Several years earlier, I encountered Jesus on a West coast midnight tidal flat. He invited me to serve others, freeing me from my twenty-something self-absorbed searching. Jesus had "saved" me from a life of serving my own needs and called me to serve his higher purpose. Not knowing exactly what that would look like—it quickened my heart—this new purpose was squeezing me like a sponge! I was young and eager to start "giving back" the privilege and blessings I'd been soaking up in church, school, and family all my life.

I landed back in Toronto and was offered a job taking small groups of homeless folks up to a derelict United Church camp for a week. There, I sat with Jesus around campfires and listened to stories, stories, and more stories. While others might have seen broken people needing fixing, Jesus gave me the eyes to see souls with gifts to offer—but without opportunity. If "it's better to give than receive," I wondered what happens to my self-esteem (if I'm only on the receiving end of charity) without any opportunities to give, to serve, to take a role in community?

The United Church of Canada was my family's church. Our family tree has plenty of clergy in its branches. While I admired the bottom-up work of overseas missionaries,

Canadian congregations served middle-class folks. Marginalized folks remained on its margins. Charity kept them alive but uninvolved in the give and take of community. While I doubted that serving Jesus—for me—would mean serving a congregation, I enrolled in theological studies. My Dad told me I needed a trade, and "church work" was an honest profession.

After a couple of years of full-time theology studies, I grew restless with all the study and talk of Christ's liberating story being lived-out by oppressed peoples in the "Third World." In Latin America, cell groups of revolutionaries studied and prayed together on the gospel vision of liberation. I needed to test it out here in Canada. Where was liberation alive where I lived? I pulled out of full-time studies and took a job offer with an inner-city mission in Toronto's east end.

My spouse of two years was working in corporate sales. Our worlds couldn't have been more different. Our common ground was a passion for the "kin-dom" of a Jesus community. She became pregnant about the same time I liberated myself from theology school. My new job was to gather homeless folks into shared, subsidized houses scattered around the downtown eastside. If I had known just how deep and wild the waters I was plunging into were, I might never have dived in. But God soon sent me a partner—someone who knew those waters well. We met as bad actors in a play about the history of Cabbagetown (a Toronto neighbourhood) in the 1930s. Sitting around waiting for our big scene, we got to talking about Jesus.

The deep creases in Ron's face were a road map of misery. But they would disappear when he broke into a wide grin, a roaring laugh, or a story—which was often. As a long-time, gospel-singing, Jesus-loving street preacher, he was more than a bit suspicious of all my book-learned faith. I told him about how God had put a dream into me. Why not start a worker co-op that would employ previously homeless folks to give them a purpose and a way to contribute? Once people had a place to live, they needed a purpose. Everyone does. For me, when Jesus said, "I have come to bring you a full life," that's what he meant: a life of both giving and receiving. The houses I was moving people into needed repairs. We could start there.

Ron had a lifetime of home repairs and contracting work behind him. He'd helped his dad and uncles build houses since he was old enough to swing a hammer. He'd also had seven wives who'd birthed a few dozen children, served in Korea, been treated with electroshock, and survived cancer and alcoholism. Ron's faith in the Almighty had taken him through the fires of hell more than a few times. His heart bore the scars. I had an arts degree, church connections, and my wife's credit card. We connected around the idea that good work would do much to heal the wounds that living on the street could inflict on a person's self-worth. He told me, "With your connections and my know-how, we'll make that dream happen."

Where did that mission come from? Nobody asked me to do it. No one was offering a paycheque. It was a seed planted in my heart. It slowly took shape in my imagination and grew in me like a pregnancy: unavoidable, uncomfortable, growing larger and larger, until it just had to be born.

To follow in the Jesus path, for me, meant creating ways to involve people from society's margins in a common purpose, in a community where respect for every person's dignity, gifts, and wounds were expressed in mutuality. My role was to invite people's gifts into service. Rich and poor. Conservative and anarchist. Religious and not. My prayer was, "You open the doors, God, and I'll walk through them."

Ron and I started praying together. It was a dangerous thing to be doing with someone like Ron. If God has a preferential option for the poor, then Ron had God's attention! I pitched the home-repair co-op idea to my boss. He told me it was impossible. But that response was like pouring gas on the fire. "With God, all things are possible," quoted Ron. God's Spirit was kicking inside of me, disturbing me into action, making me dissatisfied with band-aid work.

The vision of a community liberated from charity and founded in kinship led me to quit my job at the Mission. I bought a 1975 Ford three-quarter ton pick-up truck, and Ron and I pulled together our first crew. It was the beginning of what was to become the Handyworkers Home Repair Worker Co-op, launched with a loan from The United Church of Canada. Two years later, I was ordained and settled into the Riverdale Economic Ministry, a community ministry started by folks who shared the dream God had seeded.

My theology-school pal Nan was the first to take a risk hiring us. She needed to move so we agreed to supply the truck and a crew on June 9. The day of our first big job was also the first day my other mission started: fatherhood!

In the middle of the night, my wife Carol

cried out from the bathroom. "My water just broke!" Her cry caused me to leap up out of bed. As I rushed into the bathroom, the blood caught up to my head with a whoosh. I passed out, hitting the floor at Carol's feet! The transformation had begun. I woke on the bathroom floor with Carol bent over me. She looked concerned. I sat up, turned, and vomited my old self into the toilet.

I had to call Ron from the hospital. "You'll have to do the moving job without me. The baby's coming!" I hung up, thinking it was so good to have a partner to shift the weight onto.

Carol has her own story to tell about just how tough and scary was her delivery of Alana Sarah into the world. I was a witness to the fear and the blood, the wails and the wonder, the awe of watching mother and child together push past death's door to start a new tiny person into life's journey.

Where did this person come from? Like the mission God planted in my belly, she arrived from the ancient stream of God's abundant making. Neither depended entirely upon me, but both broke me open to depend on the Spirit's help. I was gifted with the task of shepherding, of guiding, of asking and inviting the gifts of whoever God sent our way—and then working out how God's purpose might emerge in the Spirit's offerings of chance encounters and synchronous circumstances.

On leaving the delivery room, I ran into Ron. He had a big born-again grin on his face. "What are you doing here?" I asked, surprised that he wasn't moving Nan's stuff.

"I told the boys: Al's having a baby! So take the day off." It was obvious to him that the birth of any child was good reason enough for the world to stop and celebrate!

Nan has never let me forget it. As if I ever could.

> *Allan Smith-Reeve has spent the last thirty years pursuing a ministry of bridging poverty and privilege, creating opportunities for folks from the margins to contribute. He*

serves with Greenwood United Church in Peterborough, ON, whose ministry includes www.BridgesPeterborough.ca.

An Invitation

Rob Fennell, editor

This book, and its corresponding e-book version, are a not-for-profit project. Neither the Authors nor I gain financially from its publication. Proceeds go to the Canadian Centre to End Human Trafficking.

Please support the Centre if you are able: https://www.canadiancentretoendhumantrafficking.ca/

If you are interested to read some of my other books and articles, you can find them here: https://rfennell8.wixsite.com/rcfennell

www.ingramcontent.com/pod-product-compliance
Lightning Source LLC
Chambersburg PA
CBHW031123080526
44587CB00011B/1091